100 THINGS
TO KNOW ABOUT
INVENTIONS

Author: Clive Gifford
Illustrator: Yiffy Gu
Designer: Sarah Chapman-Suire
Editor: Carly Madden
Creative Director: Malena Stojic
Publisher: Rhiannon Findlay

First published in 2021 by Happy Yak,
an imprint of The Quarto Group.
26391 Crown Valley Parkway, Suite 220,
Mission Viejo, CA 92691, USA.
T: +1 949 380 7510 F: +1 949 380 7575
www.quartoknows.com

A CIP record for this book is available from the Library of Congress.

ISBN 978 0 7112 6808 1

Manufactured in Guangdong, China TT062021

9 8 7 6 5 4 3 2 1

100 THINGS TO KNOW ABOUT INVENTIONS

CLIVE GIFFORD   YIFFY GU

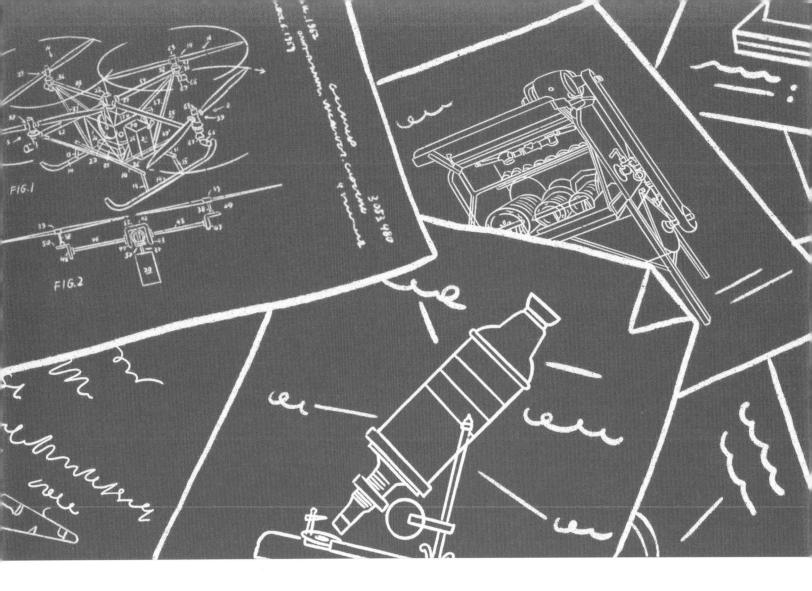

CONTENTS

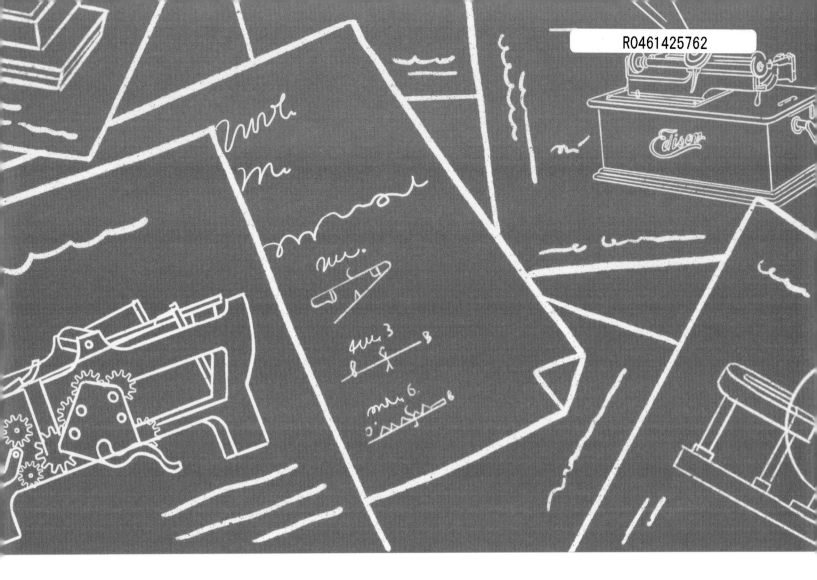

INTRODUCTION

Every day, when you switch on a light, computer, or radio, ride your bike, write a note, or open the fridge, you are using objects and materials that didn't exist centuries earlier. These inventions didn't spring out of thin air—they're all the work of ingenious, hardworking, and sometimes downright lucky inventors! Some inventions come in a sudden flash of inspiration, while others take many years of struggle to make them work. Many inventions do not succeed, but when they do they have the potential to transform the way many people live.

This book celebrates the importance of innovations by examining 100 key examples of inventions, big and small. Some have changed the world, while others have made daily life a little bit easier or more rewarding. All have fascinating and sometimes surprising stories to tell and will give you lots to think and talk about.

So what are you waiting for? The world of inventions is just a page turn away!

8

WHEEL

· ·

Many inventions evolve out of new ways of using existing things. In Mesopotamia (present day Iraq), 5,500–6,000 years ago, people created simple potters' wheels by spinning circular slabs of wood or stone positioned parallel to the ground. Around 3,500 BCE, some smart folks began placing wheels on their side and inserting a rod through the middle as an axle, so the wheel could turn. Wheels encounter far less friction than an object that is dragged across the ground, so when fitted to carts—pulled by oxen or mules—wheels made moving people, crops, and other goods around quicker and easier.

SKATES

Belgian Joseph Merlin had a smashing time when parading his new invention at a London masquerade party in 1760. He played a violin while gliding through the rooms on wheeled plates attached to his boots—a demonstration which ended abruptly with him smashing both an expensive mirror and his violin! Despite Merlin's mishap, roller skating caught on, especially after the invention of the 2x2 (or quad skates) by New York furniture dealer Joseph Plimpton in 1863. Plimpton's skates featured four wheels fitted to a plate that could lean left or right, allowing skaters to turn by shifting their body weight.

STEAM

In 1698, Englishman Thomas Savery invented an engine which produced power by boiling water, turning it into steam that expanded with force. Savery's engine and those that followed mostly worked as pumps removing water from mines. In 1764, Scotsman James Watt began a long series of major improvements to increase the power and usefulness of steam engines. In 1781, Watt invented a system that converted the straight up and down movement of a steam engine into a rotary (turning) movement, perfect for driving millwheels and other machinery. Watt's innovations transformed steam engines into versatile power sources for industry and transport.

LOOM

A loom is a machine that weaves yarn or long threads together to make cloth. In the 1760s, new machines were spinning more yarn than ever before. Edmund Cartwright devised machinery to speed up the process. He built his first basic power loom in 1784. Later versions wove cloth three times faster than a person using a handloom! Power looms were originally driven by waterwheels, but when waterwheels were replaced by steam engines, loom factories could be located anywhere, not just beside rivers. By 1850, there were 250,000 power looms at work in England alone, producing vast amounts of cloth.

CRANE

· ·

Rope running over a wheel forms a device called a pulley. When a number of pulleys are used together, people can lift heavy loads using a lot less effort! The ancient Greeks used the amazing power of pulleys to invent the first cranes in the 6th century BCE. Pulleys and ropes that were fitted to a tall, strong, wooden frame enabled heavier loads to be lifted than before, such as large stone blocks or marble statues. The Romans then developed cranes powered by people walking on large wheels. These human-powered cranes could easily lift big loads of four or more tons.

LEGO®

Danish carpenter Ole Kirk Christiansen set up *Leg Godt*, meaning "play well," in 1934. The company produced and sold wooden—and later plastic—toys. In 1949, Christiansen introduced the business's first plastic building bricks, which were redesigned as LEGO® in 1958. These hollow plastic blocks interlock due to their round studs on top, allowing infinite building combinations. Amazingly, just six eight-studded bricks can be put together in over 915 million different ways! Molded from tough plastic since 1964, more than 70 billion bricks and accessories are sold each year. Bricks made today will still work with those produced in 1958!

PLOW

Around 6,000–6,500 years ago, people in ancient Egypt began using something called an ard or scratch plow to prepare their farm fields. A stout, pointed stick was attached to a frame and pulled by cows or oxen. The stick dug into the soil and broke up hard, baked ground, bringing nutrients to the surface and letting water in. Plowing produced long, shallow furrows in which seeds could be planted. This ground-breaking tool helped increase the amount of crops grown. While more complex metal plows have since been developed, simple wooden scratch plows are still used in some places today.

LAWNMOWER

Grass was once cut very slowly using handheld scythes or grazing animals, until an English engineer spied a cylinder-shaped cloth-trimming machine in a cloth mill around 1830. Edwin Beard Budding placed a cylinder with blades at the front of what would become the first lawnmower, which linked to a roller at the back. As the mower was pushed, the roller turned, moving the cylinder and blades, which trimmed the grass. Mowers gained motors in the 1900s, and in 1995 a Swedish company introduced the first solar-powered robot lawnmower, which could cut grass by itself without anyone needing to push it!

PHOTOCOPIER

Inventing takes belief, determination, and persistence. After several years of experiments, Chester Carlson invented the electrophotography process in 1938. This used static electricity to copy an image onto a turning metal drum, which attracted powdered ink called toner. The toner then transferred the image onto plain paper and was heated to become permanent. Carlson was turned down by 20 companies before his process was taken up and renamed xerography. The first photocopier, the XeroX Model A (1948), required 39 steps to make one copy! It would be another ten years before the first easy-to-use copier, the Xerox 914, was launched.

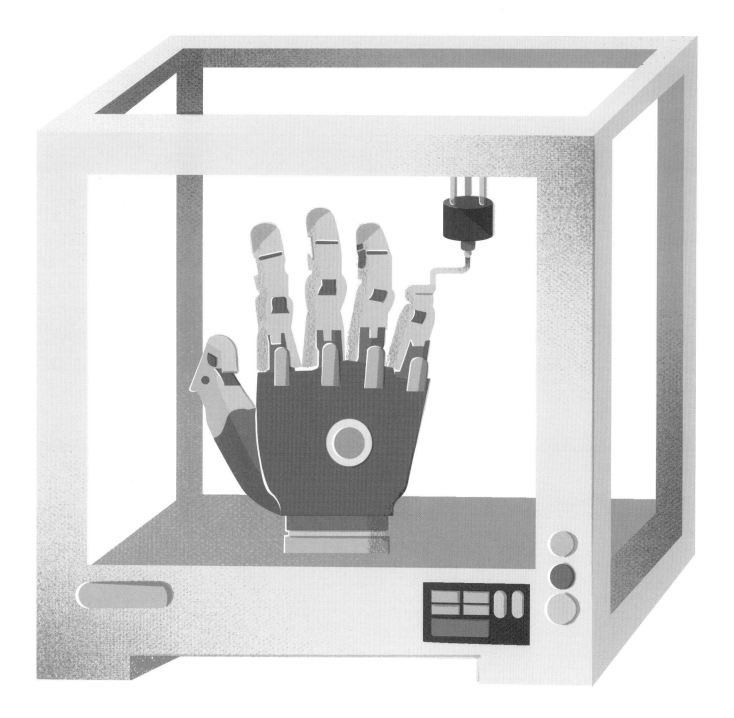

3D PRINTING

3D printers convert a digital file on a computer into a physical, solid object. Most do this by depositing layer upon layer of plastic, metal, or another material repeatedly, to build up the object. Charles "Chuck" Hull pioneered early 3D printing in the 1980s. In 1987 he co-formed a company and launched the very first 3D printer—the SLA-1. 3D printing can produce complex, intricate products with perfect accuracy, from car and aircraft components to toys and even replacement human body parts. The process has also been adopted by many inventors to produce rapid prototypes of their inventions for testing.

COMPUTER

Annoyed with how printed lists of numbers were often riddled with errors, British engineer Charles Babbage began building intricate mechanical machines in the 1820s. His engines were designed to work out answers accurately and were 100 years ahead of their time. Just like modern computers, the steam-powered Analytical Engine was programmable, could solve any calculation imaginable, and had separate parts for processing, memory, and output. Sadly, engineering issues stopped Babbage from completing his revolutionary machines. However, his friend and aspiring mathematician Ada Lovelace made a series of successful instructions for the Analytical Engine, making her the world's first computer programmer.

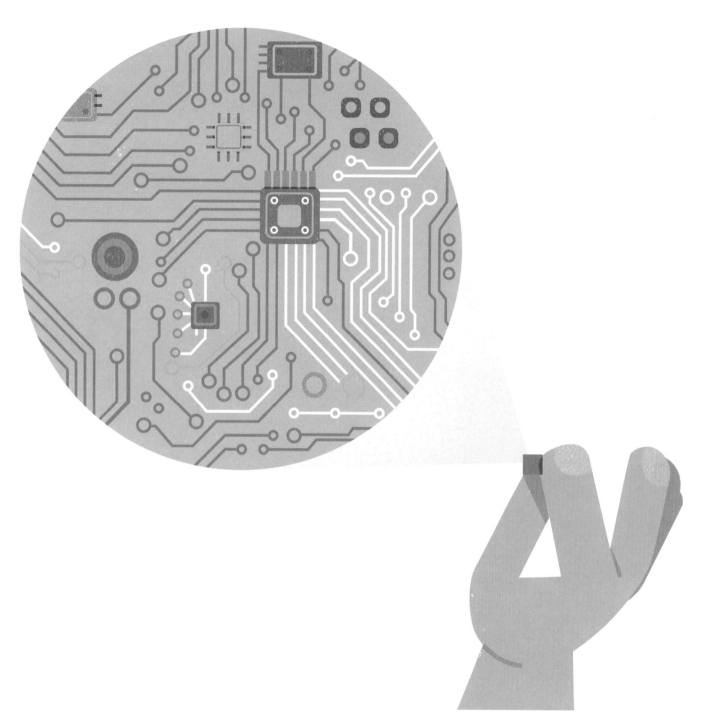

MICROCHIP

The first electronic computers in the 1940s weighed many tons, filled entire rooms, and contained miles of wiring. In 1947, a tiny electronic switch—the transistor—was invented, enabling smaller, faster circuits to be constructed. Engineer Jack Kilby aimed to shrink things further by eliminating wiring and making microscopic circuits and their parts out of just a single, tiny wafer of semiconducting material. Kilby patented his integrated circuit, known as a microchip, in 1959. Another US engineer, Robert Noyce, helped simplify the production of microchips, and the result was a boom in computing with smaller, cheaper, and more powerful computers.

PATENT

Behind even the simplest of inventions may lie months or years of effort. Patents are ways inventors can protect their work. Inventors submit their ideas and, if successful, patents are granted by governments for a set period of time. Others are not allowed to copy the invention until the patent expires. Once expired, anyone can use the information. Serial inventor Thomas Edison took out 1,093 US patents, but not all led to successful products. Many patented inventions stay on the drawing board until the technology to make them catches up, such as Edward Vanderlip's 1962 pioneering patent for quadcopter drones.

SAFETY PIN

Mechanical mastermind Walter Hunt created sewing machines, saws, bicycles ... even shoes that let circus performers walk up walls! A better inventor than businessman, Hunt found himself in debt in 1849. While fiddling in his workshop he discovered how he could coil wire into a spring and hinge, with the two wire ends forming a pin and clasp. In a flash, a single piece of wire could be turned cheaply into a complete, safely-locking pin. Hunt obtained a patent in April 1849 but immediately sold it for $400. Millions upon millions of these handy everyday objects have been manufactured ever since.

VACUUM

· ·

After watching a new dust-blowing cleaning machine invented in 1901, Hubert Cecil Booth wondered why the machine didn't capture the dust rather than blow it around! Booth built his Puffing Billy vacuum cleaner the same year. It featured a gasoline engine-powered pump, which sucked in air and dust. The machine was so large that it had to be parked outside houses and its suction tubes carried in through doors and windows! Booth fitted transparent tubes so customers could witness the dust leaving their home. Booth's machines proved a hit with wealthy Londoners who even hired them for vacuum cleaning parties!

REFRIGERATOR

Refrigerators generate low temperatures, which slow the growth of bacteria that cause food to spoil. Their development began in 1748, when Scotsman William Cullen demonstrated how liquid expanding into gas draws heat away from its surroundings. This process—evaporative cooling—was finally applied over 100 years later in large machines and used in the meat, fish, and dairy industries. Home refrigerators didn't arrive until the 20th century. Fred Wolf's 1913 refrigerator was unsuccessful but its ice cube tray would be adopted by the many fridges that quickly followed. By 1920, 200 different refrigerator models were available in the US alone.

PHOTOGRAPHY

· ·

The oldest surviving photograph was made in 1826 by French inventor Nicéphore Niépce, using a sheet of pewter coated in sticky bitumen, which reacted to light. By 1839, Louis Daguerre developed metal plates coated in silver compounds. His "daguerreotypes" proved popular for portrait photographs, even though cameras were large and people had to sit still for many minutes. In the 1880s, George Eastman perfected a cheaper, more portable method by recording images onto a roll of flexible film, coated with light-sensitive chemicals. His first Kodak box camera using these film rolls launched in 1888. Suddenly everyone could now take photos!

DIGITAL CAMERA

Taking photographs without film became possible once engineer Steve Sasson helped develop a new sensor—the charged couple device (CCD). This converted light into electrical signals which were processed into a digital image. Sasson built a camera using a CCD, some movie camera parts, and a tape machine. Each small black and white image the camera captured took 23 seconds to record onto audiocassette. Digital cameras weren't on sale until the 1990s or used in mobile phones until the 2000s. Today, many smartphones contain three or more cameras, each capable of capturing 20,000 times more detail than Sasson's original device.

BALLOON

Dreams of human flight were first made a reality in France. Balloonists soared in cloth and paper balloons filled with heated air or hydrogen gas—both gases lighter than the surrounding air. French paper mill owners Joseph-Michel and Jacques-Étienne Montgolfier experimented by sending up a duck, rooster, and sheep in 1783! It was an eight minute flight watched by a crowd of over 130,000. Next, the brothers constructed a 46-foot diameter balloon, beneath which straw burned in an iron basket to heat the air. It transported a chemistry teacher and a soldier on a pioneering 25 minute flight above Paris.

SUBMARINE

Dutchman Cornelis Drebbel is believed to have built the very first submarine in 1620—a covered rowing boat that was tested in London's River Thames. Attempts to make more practical vessels didn't flourish until the late-19th century, when Irishman J.P. Holland made a series of inventive submarines. His 1897 vessel *Holland* was powered by an electric motor underwater, and a gasoline engine on the surface. The 20th century saw large military submarines and smaller civilian submersibles explore underwater. They discovered unknown plants and creatures, and plane and shipwrecks. The submarine *Trieste* reached the deepest part of the ocean in 1960.

WRITING

Written language to record information and express ideas was invented independently in many locations, including China (c.1300 BCE) and Egypt (c.3200 BCE). The ancient Sumerian system called cuneiform extends back further (c.3400–3500 BCE). It began as pictures and symbols, but developed into a system of characters, each representing a spoken language sound. The Sumerians used a stylus, made from a frayed river reed, to press characters into soft clay tablets. The completed tablets were dried and hardened in the sun. Cuneiform was initially written vertically but later in left-to-right rows. Today, Korean, Chinese, and Japanese can be written either horizontally or vertically.

BRAILLE

In 1824, a 15-year-old blind French boy, Louis Braille, developed an ingenious touch-reading system for those who couldn't see. Braille's system consisted of up to six raised dots in a small 3x2 grid called a cell. The position and number of dots could produce 64 different combinations, enough to represent each letter of the alphabet, basic punctuation, and the numbers 0–9. With cells small enough for each character to be identified using a single fingertip, people learned to read text written in braille quickly. Today, braille books are accompanied by braille signs, typewriters, and printers, all helping the visually impaired.

CAR

Steam-powered carriages were first attempted in 1769, but practical road vehicles needed a more lightweight and reliable source of power. German engineer Carl Benz fitted an internal combustion engine—which burned air and fuel inside small cylinders—to his three-wheeled Patent-Motorwagen in 1885. The car had a top speed of 16 kph and was maneuvered by a tiller (lever) rather than a steering wheel. In 1888, Benz's intrepid wife, Bertha, along with their sons, drove 112 miles between Mannheim and Pforzheim—the first road trip. On the drive, she had to buy fuel from pharmacies as gas stations hadn't yet been invented!

TRAFFIC LIGHTS

· ·

In 1868, the world's first road traffic lights were installed outside the Houses of Parliament in London. The gas-powered lights, designed by John Peake Knight, unfortunately exploded the following year and London's next set didn't arrive until 1925! Electric traffic lights were invented in the US, where booming cities and increasing motor vehicle use meant chaotic road junctions and many accidents. Salt Lake City policeman Lester Wire invented a two-lens traffic light in 1912, which took power from overhead trolley cables. Eight years later, a Detroit police officer, William Potts, invented the three-lens light with yellow between red and green.

PAPER

Writing was produced on clay tablets, silk, papyrus, or animal skin before a new material was invented in China. Paper was created by the court official Cai Lun in 105 CE. It was made by pulping plant and, later, cloth fibers together, soaking them in water, and pressing them against a mesh screen to form a thin layer. Once dry, the material accepted ink well, was lighter than bamboo and cheaper than silk. China kept its paper-making secret from the world and it took more than 500 years before the invention spread, first to Korea and Japan, then the Arab world.

PENCIL

In 1564, a huge deposit of solid graphite was discovered in Borrowdale, north-western England. Looking like coal but leaving a strong black mark, chunks were first used by shepherds to mark their sheep. Later, pieces were sawn off and wrapped in string or sheepskin to make invaluable drawing tools. A shortage of solid graphite in 1790s France prompted Nicholas-Jacques Conté to oven bake graphite powder mixed with clay, before wrapping the thin leads in wood—making the first pencils! By varying the mixture, Conté made pencils of differing blackness and hardness from 9B to 9H—a system still used today.

BATTERY

In 1799, Italian Alessandro Volta created the first chemical store of electricity—called a "voltaic pile." It consisted of alternate discs of zinc and copper or silver, with a sandwich of brine-soaked cardboard in between. Volta had discovered when certain metals were submerged in acid, a small electric current was generated. He demonstrated his invention in London in 1800 and to the French ruler, Napoleon, the following year. Over time, more practical batteries were developed but the voltaic pile was copied by many scientists, who helped advance research into electricity. The electric unit of measurement, volt, is named after Alessandro.

GENERATOR

· ·

A generator converts movement (mechanical energy) into electricity. The idea behind
how a generator works was discovered by British scientist Michael Faraday in 1831. He found
that a magnet moving inside a wire coil could produce an electric current. He then built and
demonstrated a simple form of generator using a horseshoe magnet and a copper disc, which
turned between the poles of the magnet, generating a weak electric current. Faraday's innovation
was seized upon by others who produced more powerful and practical generators. Today, all the
world's electricity produced by coal, oil, wind, water, and nuclear power uses generators.

TOILET

· ·

More than 4,000 years ago, the Indus Valley (South Asia) cities of Mohenjo-Dara and
Harappa developed sophisticated sewer systems, with toilets carrying waste away thanks
to constant flowing water. The first known flushing toilet, however, was a Tudor invention.
Between 1584 and 1591, Queen Elizabeth I's godson, Sir John Harington, invented a toilet
he named Ajax. It featured a water tank called a cistern, which released a gush of water (about
8 gallons' worth!) downward to wash all the waste in the bowl away. Despite installing a version
in Queen Elizabeth's palace, Harington's invention didn't catch on for several centuries.

TOOTHBRUSH

Over 5,000 years ago, ancient Babylonians chewed frayed ends of twigs to remove food from their teeth. These chew sticks are still used in parts of Asia, where the first toothbrushes were invented during China's Tang Dynasty (619–907 CE). Tufts of hairs from Siberian pigs were embedded in handles made of bamboo or bone. In Europe, toothbrushes were rare until a prisoner in a London jail made a simple version. William Addis used a bone saved from a meal and poked bristles through small holes. When free in 1780, Addis began mass-producing toothbrushes using pig, horse, and, later, badger hair!

TELEGRAPH

Telegraphs send electric signals along wires, enabling messaging over long distances. Charles Wheatstone and William Cooke's telegraph was first used along British railway lines from 1839. In 1945, a telegraph message from Slough station to Paddington station helped police capture a murderer as he left his train! Over in America, Samuel Morse and Arthur Vail developed a clever telegraph and code system using short (dots) and long (dashes) pulses of electric signals to represent the alphabet. This "Morse Code" helped telegraph operators send messages faster— telegraphs boomed and by 1900, 63 million telegraph messages were sent in the US alone.

INTERNET

· ·

The Internet is a worldwide web of computer networks. It lets billions of computers and smartphones connect with each other. This means you can chat, message, view photos and videos, and read webpages from all over the world in seconds! No one person invented the Internet. Instead, it grew out of computing advances in the 1960s. In 1969, ARPANET was created in the United States. This network started with just four computers linked together. Gradually, more computers joined or formed their own networks elsewhere. As the networks communicated with one another and used apps like emails, the Internet was born!

CRASH TEST DUMMY

Sandbags, dead bodies, or even live human volunteers were used to play the part of crash victims, until Samuel W. Alderson created the first realistic human dummy out of rubber and steel in 1949. "Sierra Sam" was used to test pilot helmets, harnesses, and aircraft ejection seats. Today, crash test dummies are manufactured in a wide range of heights and weights to reflect the variety in human society. They are lifelike human models fitted with instruments that measure forces in crash testing and safety research. Dummies used in motor vehicle safety testing helped to develop airbags and other safety breakthroughs.

SEAT BELT

Early seat belts were single straps across the hips, but these didn't stop heads and chests from lurching forward dangerously during crashes. In 1958, Swedish engineer Nils Bohlin from car manufacturer Volvo was inspired to make improvements after his time working on pilot harnesses. His three-point seat belt added a diagonal strap across the chest, which fitted into a hip buckle that could be fastened with one hand. Volvo chose to publicize rather than patent the invention, allowing other manufacturers to copy Bohlin's simple solution. Three-point belts have saved thousands of lives and halve the risk of injury in crashes.

CONSOLE

In 1967–68, American engineer Ralph Baer invented the first computer game consoles. The system plugged into a TV's aerial socket and displayed a range of simple games in black and white. It included twist knob controls for two players and had games such as checkers, volleyball, golf putting, and table tennis—some of which were copied by competitors. Baer also created handheld light guns that detected white blocks on the screen, which were used to play a target shooting game. When the console went on sale as the Magnavox Odyssey in 1972, it marked the start of home gaming.

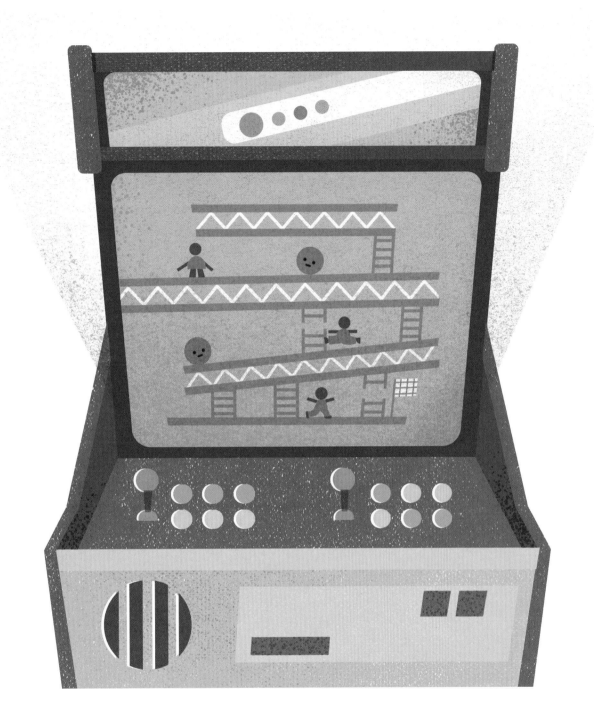

ARCADE

In 1962, US university students invented the first popular computer action game,
Spacewar! It featured two battling spaceships and was a big hit. Nolan Bushnell was an
avid Spacewar! gamer and in 1971, he and Ted Dabney created their own version, playable
in coin-operated arcades, called Computer Space. The pair formed Atari in 1972, making
successful arcade games such as Pong and Breakout. Inspired by Atari, Japan's Tomohiro Nishikado
designed Space Invaders in 1978. It became really popular with eight million daily players in
Japan alone, and was the first arcade game with a music soundtrack and high score leaderboard.

AIRCRAFT

· ·

American brothers Orville and Wilbur Wright ran a bicycle business, but were also passionate about flying. The pair studied the forces of flight, built their own wind tunnel, and made over 200 flights in their self-built gliders. In 1903, the Wrights built a 21-foot long aircraft with two sets of wings to provide lift. Forward motion was provided by a gasoline engine, which spun two 8-foot-long propellers. Orville successfully piloted the plane, while lying on his stomach, to make the first ever controlled, powered flight! In 1908, the brothers demonstrated their aircraft in Europe, sparking a huge boom in aviation.

PARACHUTE

· ·

A parachute slows the movement of an object by creating lots of drag. Parachutes are used not only to slow a descent to the ground, but also as brakes for dragster cars and some jet aircraft. Leonardo da Vinci sketched out a practical, pyramid-shaped parachute design back in 1485, but the first successful jump was made in 1783. Louis-Sebastien Lenormand leapt from Montpellier Observatory's tower, suspended beneath a cloth-covered wooden frame. Another Frenchman, André-Jacques Garnerin, invented the frameless parachute. Using his cloth canopy, Garnerin made daring descents from 2,950 feet above Paris in 1797, and 8,000 feet above London five years later.

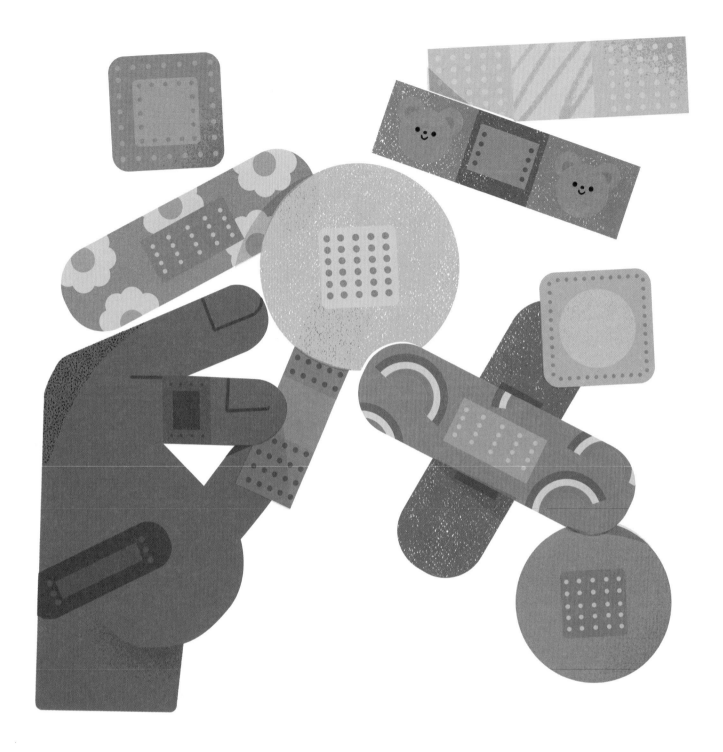

ADHESIVE BANDAGE

Cuts, burns, and grazes used to require bulky bandages and dressings that were hard to apply without someone else's help. In 1920, Johnson & Johnson employee Earle Dickson had a brainwave. He stuck a series of small, folded gauze pads at intervals along long strips of sticky tape and covered the remaining tape with crinoline fabric. Dickson's pre-made adhesive bandages could be cut off the roll and applied one-handed. His employers were impressed and Band-Aids® went on sale in 1921. Three years later, individual bandages of different shapes and sizes were first produced and are now sold and used worldwide.

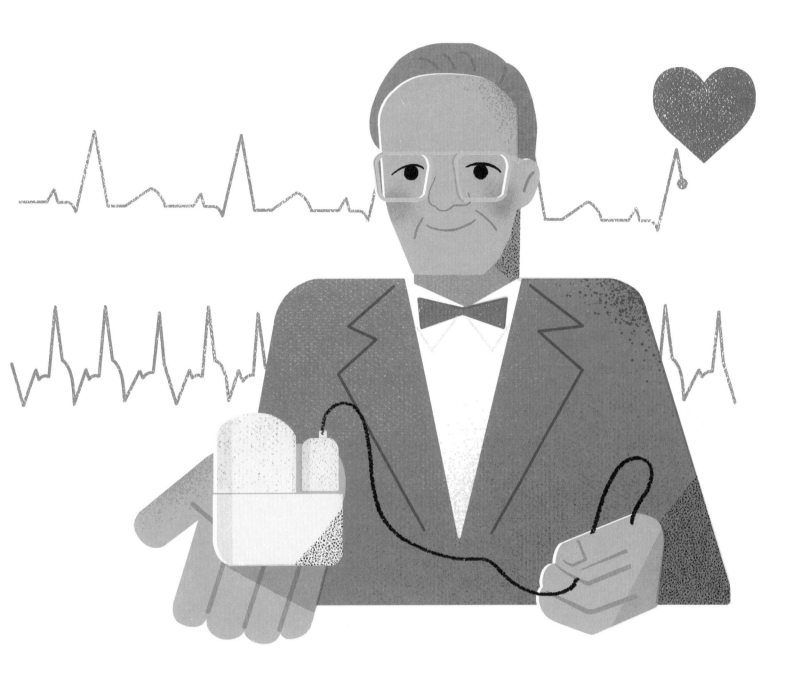

PACEMAKER

Some people's hearts do not beat regularly, which can be dangerous. Devices called pacemakers send out electrical signals at regular intervals to correct this. The first pacemaker, the size of a toaster, was invented by John Hopps in 1950. Six years later, Wilson Greatbatch fitted the wrong part to an electrical circuit and found it emitted a steady regular electrical pulse, just like a heartbeat. Working with William Chardack in 1960, the pair produced a pacemaker small enough to fit inside the body. A constant tinkerer with 330 patents, Greatbatch invented longer-lasting pacemaker batteries, which helped save thousands of lives.

CHOCOLATE

· ·

Chocolate comes from the dried and roasted beans of the cacao tree. American civilizations like the Incas, Maya, and Aztecs made a dark, bitter drink from the beans, mixed with spices and even chillis. The Aztecs called it *xocolãtl*, which later became chocolate in Spain, after 16th century explorers returned home with cacao beans. A fashion for expensive chocolate drinks sweetened with sugar spread through Europe. Cheaper chocolate came with the 1828 invention of cocoa powder, by Dutch chemist Coenraad van Houten. In 1847, Englishman Joseph Fry mixed this with cocoa butter and sugar to create the first solid chocolate.

DYE

· ·

In 1856, eighteen-year-old William Henry Perkin was toiling away in his home chemistry lab in London. He was trying to make quinine—a valuable drug used to treat malaria. Perkin failed but produced something remarkable instead—the first artificial dye, which he called mauveine. At the time, purple dyes were difficult and expensive to produce; just one gram of fancy purple dye, for example, required around 9,000 crushed tiny sea snails! Instead, mauveine was made from inexpensive coal tar, didn't fade, and sparked a fashion for purple clothing. An entire industry sprang up to produce artificial dyes in different colors.

JET

A jet engine sucks air into a combustion chamber where it is mixed with fuel and set alight. The burning mixture produces large amounts of gases, which expand rapidly backward producing forward thrust. Aircraft powered by jet engines fly faster and higher than propeller-powered planes. Two engineers—Frank Whittle in England and Hans von Ohain in Germany—both invented working jet engines in 1937. Whittle's was tested first, but von Ohain's engine became the first to power an aircraft, the *Heinkel He 178*, in 1939. Ten years later, the first jet airliner, the *de Havilland Comet*, took to the skies.

ROCKET

Rockets are self-contained engines which burn fuel and oxygen, or an oxygen-making chemical called an oxidizer. The very first rockets were simple bamboo tubes filled with gunpowder in China around 1,000 years ago. The first rocket powered by liquid fuel was launched by Robert Goddard in 1926. It only flew 200 feet, landing in a cabbage patch, but it kickstarted a boom in rocket science. Missiles powered by rocket engines appeared during World War II and early space rockets were derived from these weapons. In 1957, a Soviet R7 rocket designed by Sergei Korolev launched the first satellite into space.

FROZEN FOOD

American naturalist Clarence Birdseye was working in the Arctic in 1912–14, when he noticed how fish caught by Inuit people froze rapidly at low temperatures (-22 °F or below). This fast freezing created smaller ice crystals inside food. As a result, the thawed food's taste and texture was almost as good as fresh. Determined to mechanize the process, Birdseye spent the next decade developing flash-freezing machines. His 1924 double belt system froze food in waxed cardboard cartons, between chilled stainless steel belts. Five years later, Birdseye's flash-frozen foods first entered freezers in shops. Fish fingers didn't arrive until the 1950s!

MICROWAVE

While walking past a magnetron device at work in 1945, engineer Percy Spencer made a surprising discovery—the snack bar in his shirt pocket started melting! Magnetrons produce a type of electromagnetic radiation called microwaves. Spencer decided to carry out further experiments with food, finding raw eggs exploded and corn kernels popped! The microwaves were vibrating molecules inside food, causing them to heat up. The company Spencer worked for launched the first microwave oven in 1947. Called the Radarange, it weighed 750 pounds and stood as tall as a person! The first table top-sized microwave oven was produced in 1967.

PRINTING

Woodblock printing began in ancient China, with a single wooden block carved with a page of symbols. Around 800–900 years ago, individual symbol blocks made of clay or bronze were produced in China and Korea. These movable type blocks could be rearranged to print different pages of a book. Then, in 15th century Germany, Johannes Gutenberg developed Europe's first movable type printing press. Metal alloy type was arranged then covered with ink that stuck to the type. Pages could be printed quickly and cheaply. Gutenberg's invention was copied widely, book production soared, and information became more widespread than ever.

WORLD WIDE WEB

The World Wide Web (WWW) is a giant collection of documents known as webpages.
A group of webpages together form a website and today there are over a billion websites
across the Internet. Back in 1991, there was just one, created by British computer engineer
Tim Berners-Lee. He dreamed of building an easy way to link and access information held
on the world's computers using hyperlinks. Clicking on a hyperlink lets you jump from one
webpage to another quickly. Berners-Lee created a language to make webpages called
HTML and a browser program to view webpages on computers. Web-surfing had begun!

SEARCH ENGINE

As the amount of information grew on the Internet, it became harder to find what you needed. In 1989–90, Canada's Alan Emtage invented the first computer program that searched the Internet for content. Called Archie, it inspired other search engines, including Veronica in 1992 and Yahoo! in 1994. Two years later, Stanford University students Sergey Brin and Larry Page began BackRub. This search engine aimed to explore more webpages than before and analyze webpage links in an attempt to return more useful and relevant search results. By 1998, BackRub had developed into Google—the world's most popular search engine.

TRAIN

Trains emerged in Britain in 1802 when Richard Trevithick invented a high-pressure steam engine able to turn wheels and propel itself along tracks. Early steam railways used similar locomotives to haul heavy loads slowly at mines and ironworks. George Stephenson's Locomotion No.1 and No.2 were the first trains to carry passengers on a public railway in 1825. Stephenson's son, Robert, built the Rocket locomotive, which reached unheard of speeds of 29 mph. It operated on the world's first inter-city railway line (Liverpool–Manchester) from 1830. Railways boomed globally; by 1860, for example, the US possessed over 30,500 miles of railway lines.

PAPER BAG

Margaret Knight loved solving problems even as a child. She was only 12 when she invented a safety device later used in some American cloth-making factories. In 1868, she began working in a factory herself, one that made V-shaped paper bags with narrow bottoms. Knight cleverly reasoned that a bag with a flat, rectangular bottom could hold more, and created a machine to produce her new design of bag. She had to fight a battle in the law courts to stop her invention being copied, but won in 1868. After that, her flat-bottomed bags were found in many American stores.

COIN

· ·

During the period 650–550 BCE, the kings of Lydia (in present day Turkey) became the first known rulers to issue coins. These bean-shaped pieces of electrum (an alloy of gold and silver) were stamped with a lion's head—a symbol of the kingdom. Each coin weighed about the same and held the same value. This meant there was no need to weigh and check them repeatedly, as was the case with the gold and silver bars used in trade at the time. Coins proved a popular and portable form of money and neighboring Mediterranean states soon began producing their own coins.

SMARTPHONE

The first mobile phone, the DynaTAC 8000x, went on sale in 1983. Early mobiles were bulky and used only for voice calls. As technology developed, it became possible to cram in more circuits and components to perform other tasks. The first smartphone was called SIMON and was first demonstrated in 1992. It featured a touchscreen instead of number buttons and contained programs and applications not found in phones before, including a calendar, an email app, and a sketchpad program. The 8-inch-tall phone weighed 18 ounces, and contained just 1 MB of memory. A typical smartphone today boasts 64,000 times more!

EMOJI

Emojis are single character pictures that convey an idea or feeling. Before emojis, there were emoticons—combinations of regular keyboard characters such as :-) for a smiley face. These were first presented by US academic Scott Fahlman in 1982. In 1995, a Japanese telecommunications company offered the very first emoji—a heart symbol—for users of its paging service. Noting its popularity, one employee, Shigetaka Kurita, designed 176 color characters, each measuring a few pixels, to convey messages quickly, using less data. Kurita's emojis debuted on phones in 1999 and proved popular. Thousands of new emojis have since been created.

SUPERGLUE

. . . .

This fast-acting glue was discovered accidentally not once but twice! In 1942, American chemist Dr. Harry Coover was trying to make see-through plastics when he stumbled across a very sticky substance. He forgot all about it, only for his colleague to rediscover it again in 1951. The substance could make a powerful glue that bonded items almost instantly and was first launched in 1958, with a far from "super" name—Eastman #910.

In 2015, a Russian TV show demonstrated the glue's strength by dangling a man upside-down from a high-flying balloon, with only his shoes superglued to a wooden plank!

POST-IT® NOTE

Some inventions have to wait a little while to find their place in the world!
This was the case with ACM—a type of glue developed by American chemist
Dr. Spencer Silver in 1968. Silver's new glue gripped paper but could be pulled away
easily and re-stuck, again and again. Few useful tasks were found for this glue until
1974, when a fellow scientist and colleague, Art Fry, used the adhesive on paper strips
to mark places inside his choir's hymn books. Quickly realizing the potential of sticky
paper notes as bookmarks and reminders, Post-It® Notes were launched in 1980.

SCUBA

In 1943, French explorer Jacques Cousteau made the first dive using a device that would transform underwater exploration. It consisted of air tanks worn on a diver's back, which fed compressed air through a special valve. The valve, made by Cousteau's friend Émile Gagnan, matched the air's pressure to the surrounding water pressure. This stopped the diver's lungs from being harmed. Gagnan and Cousteau's self-contained underwater breathing apparatus (SCUBA for short and also known as an aqualung) was a huge success. Divers could now explore freely without being restrained by air tubes running from their helmet to a surface ship.

SPACECRAFT

After his success with rockets and satellites, Sergei Korolev was challenged by the Soviet Union government to send humans into space … and return them safely! Korolev and a team of thousands developed the Vostok spacecraft. It featured an equipment module with a rocket engine, and a 7.5 foot-wide sphere in which an astronaut lay strapped to their seat. In 1961, Yuri Gagarin became the first person in space, parachuting safely back to Earth after a 108-minute spaceflight aboard *Vostok 1*. Vostok spacecraft would fly five more successful missions. The last, in 1963, saw Valentina Tereshkova become the first woman in space.

LIGHT BULB

The first practical electrical lighting relied on incandescent light bulbs. These contain a thin filament of material that heats up, glows, and emits light when electricity passes through. To stop the filament catching fire, the bulbs need to be emptied of air, a tricky process back then. In 1880, English scientist Joseph Swan demonstrated his airtight light bulbs (with cotton filaments) by first lighting a building (his home), then an entire street in Newcastle, England. Thomas Edison was also making light bulbs with longer-lasting filaments. In 1883, Edison and Swan formed a company to make electric lighting available for everyone.

FILAMENT

Lewis Latimer, the son of an African-American slave, joined the US Navy at age 15 and later taught himself technical drawing while working at a law firm. Latimer produced the patent drawings for Alexander Graham Bell's telephone and in 1884 was hired by light bulb expert Thomas Edison. Two years earlier, he had filed his own patent for creating more durable filaments—the part of a light bulb that heats up and gives off light when electricity passes through. Latimer's carbon filaments could be manufactured more easily and lasted longer than other types. They were quickly adopted in many lights.

FIREWORK

Over 1,200 years ago, people in ancient China made an explosive discovery. Blending sulfur, charcoal, and saltpeter (potassium nitrate) in the right amounts resulted in a mixture that burned fiercely or exploded when lit. The substance was a form of gunpowder, and when packed into bamboo tubes and set light to, it created the very first firework. By the 1500s, fireworks were enjoyed in Europe too but remained a dull, white-yellow color. In the 1830s, Italian chemists added potassium chlorate to make fireworks burn brighter, and metal salts to create different colors, including copper (blue), strontium (red), and barium (green).

NEON

In 1902, French chemical engineer Georges Claude discovered that passing an electric current through a sealed glass tube containing neon produced an orange-red light. Other gases such as argon produced different colors. An advertising agent, Jacques Fonseque, saw the potential to produce colored lit signs from glass tubes, shaped into letters and symbols. The pair then first displayed their neon lights in 1910 and two years later sold their first sign to a barber shop in Paris. The world's largest neon sign was unveiled in 1984. This 125-foot-wide sign for an American hotel contained over 3.7 miles of neon tubes.

AIRSHIP

Hot-air and hydrogen balloons could only travel in the direction the wind carried them. That changed in 1852 when Frenchman Henri Giffard built the first powered, steerable balloon—an airship. It featured a 144-foot-long hydrogen balloon, beneath which a lightweight steam engine turned a propeller 110 times a minute. Giffard's invention inspired others, including Ferdinand von Zeppelin, whose LZ1 ship flew in 1900. It was the first rigid airship—a craft containing many bags of gas surrounded by a strong frame. Later airships built by Zeppelin (also known as Zeppelins) were used by the military and to carry civilian passengers.

HELICOPTER

Helicopters generate lift by turning rotor blades, which act like wings as they spin through the air. Prototypes were built in the 1930s but it was Russian Igor Sikorsky who mastered how to keep a helicopter stable when flying. In 1939, his VS-300 helicopter made its first flight, with Sikorsky at the controls. The helicopter featured a set of three main rotor blades and two sets of smaller rotors on its tail. These balanced out the spinning of the main rotor blades and enabled the helicopter to steer. Within four years, Sikorsky helicopters were serving in the US Air Force.

RADIO WAVES

Many people were involved in the discovery and use of radio waves. These included Nikola Tesla, who in 1898 invented the first radio-controlled device, a model boat, and Reginald Fessenden, who made the first public radio broadcast of music in 1906. Radio waves were used by Guglielmo Marconi to send and receive telegraph signals without wires. In 1901, he managed to send a signal across the Atlantic Ocean. It wasn't long before ships were equipped with radio telegraphs. One such device, aboard the *RMS Republic*, sent a distress call in 1909 that led to the rescue of over 1,500 people.

TELEVISION

· ·

TV has no single inventor. Many pioneers all strived to transmit pictures and sound through the air to be received and viewed on television sets. These included American teenager Philo Farnsworth, Japan's Kenjiro Takayanagi, and Scotsman John Logie Baird. In 1925–26, Baird produced the first television pictures showing alphabet letters and a ventriloquist's dummy! Four years later, he began broadcasting three half-hour TV shows a week. Baird's mechanical TV system was soon overtaken by electronic television sets such as those developed by Russian-American Vladimir Zworykin. These used a device called a cathode ray tube to display images much more clearly.

TELESCOPE

In 1608, Dutch eyeglasses maker Hans Lippershey placed two glass lenses in a tube. Peering through one end, he discovered far away objects appeared two to three times closer. News of Lippershey's invention reached Italian scientist Galileo Galilei, who built telescopes of his own but with a greater magnifying power. Galileo used his telescopes to make a number of astronomical advances in 1609–10, including measuring craters on the Moon and the discovery of four moons orbiting the planet Jupiter. Sixty years later, Sir Isaac Newton invented a whole new type of telescope, the reflector, which used mirrors instead of lenses.

MICROSCOPE

Like telescopes, microscopes began with Dutch lens makers. In the 1590s, Hans and Zacharias Janssen used glass lenses to magnify the view of small objects. The microscope was considered a novelty until the 1660s when improved versions were used by Englishman Robert Hooke to explore as yet unseen worlds. Hooke discovered that plants were made of building blocks— which he named cells—and his book *Micrographia* became the first science bestseller. It inspired Dutchman Antonie van Leeuwenhoek to produce microscopes with tiny, highly curved lenses and up to 270x magnification power, which he used to discover bacteria in the 1670s.

MICROCOMPUTER

While designing an electronic calculator, engineers Ted Hoff and Federico Faggin squeezed all the circuits and functions of a computer onto a single microchip. Their invention was released in 1971 as the Intel 4004 microprocessor. This, along with innovations including Random Access Memory (RAM) in 1968, meant that smaller, cheaper personal computers—microcomputers— could be constructed. The French Micral N microcomputer in 1973 was first, followed by a range of different machines. Some, like the Altair 8800, came as kits. Later models like the Apple II and TRS-80 were more user-friendly and brought computing into homes for the first time.

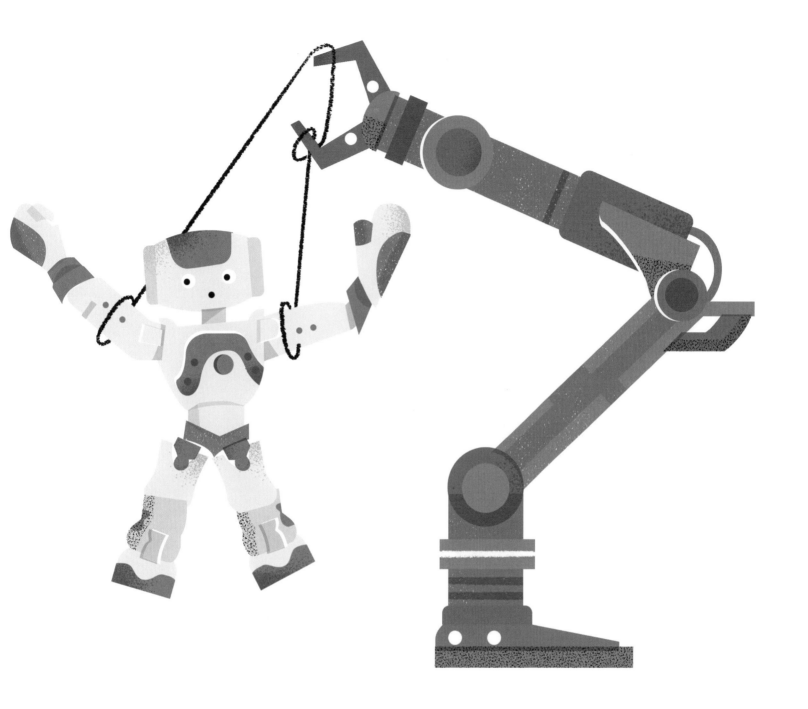

ROBOT

A robot is a versatile, programmable machine able to make decisions so it can perform tasks with little or no human help. The first working robot was installed in a car factory in 1961. This Unimate #001 robot, devised by George Devol and Joseph Engelberger, handled red hot metal tirelessly for many years. Millions of robots have since followed, many equipped with computing power so they can make their own decisions. Robots are exploring Mars and Earth's oceans. They're helping to perform life-saving operations, fight fires, and deal with unexploded bombs. Some act as home helpers, vacuum cleaners, and security guards!

BICYCLE

Bicycles emerged in 1817 when Karl von Drais invented his Laufmaschine. Riders propelled this two-wheeled wooden vehicle by paddling their feet on the ground. By the 1860s, paddling had been replaced by pedals fitted to the front wheel. Some of these wheels grew to extraordinary sizes; France's Eugène Meyer and Englishman James Starley built penny farthing bicycles with front wheels up to 4 feet in diameter. Starley's nephew, John, introduced the safety bicycle in 1885. It boasted a diamond-shaped frame, handlebars, and pedals below the rider, turning the rear wheel via a chain and chainwheel—all features of bikes today.

KEVLAR®

In the 1960s, US chemist Stephanie Kwolek was seeking out new materials able to perform well in extreme conditions to strengthen car tires. Working at a chemicals company, Kwolek produced a new, stiff plastic fiber, which became known as Kevlar®. The new material was very light in weight but extremely strong—more than five times stronger than steel. It could also withstand extreme cold and heat up to 450 °C. Kevlar® now stiffens and reinforces many objects—from tires to tennis rackets—and its use in crash helmets, body armor, gloves, and other safety equipment has saved thousands of lives.

STAMP

. . . .

Postal services have existed for centuries but many early systems were haphazard and confusing. Costs could vary wildly in different local areas and charges were often paid by the receiver, not the sender. British postal reformer Rowland Hill suggested a single, nationwide charge for letters up to 14 grams, paid by the sender. Proof of payment was a paper rectangle stuck to the letter—a postage stamp. The world's first national postage stamp, the Penny Black, went on UK sale in 1840. Its success encouraged other nations, like Brazil in 1843 and the US in 1847, to introduce their own.

BUBBLE WRAP

Working in a garage in 1957, US engineer Alfred Fielding and Swiss chemist Marc Chavannes trapped air bubbles between layers of plastic sheeting. The pair believed they had invented exciting, futuristic wallpaper but few buyers came forward. So, they repurposed their bubble-filled plastic as insulation for greenhouses! Again, there was little commercial interest. Persevering, the pair marketed the plastic sheeting as a packaging solution. The bubbles of air cushioned delicate objects without adding much weight. Computing companies were early customers, using the plastic to protect delicate technology. Millions of yards are now produced, particularly for food packaging and padded envelopes.

TIMEKEEPING

The earliest time-measuring devices were shadow sticks. These upright poles measured the Sun's daily movement across the sky by casting shadows on the ground. Sundials work in a similar way. Both, though, are of little use when it's cloudy or dark, so some people learned to measure time using the melting of a burning candle or water dripping steadily between two bowls. By 1400 BCE, ancient Egyptians built clepsydras (water clocks). Ancient Muslim and Chinese clepsydras featured elaborate mechanisms with moving figures powered by water. Mechanical clocks that used slowly falling weights and uncoiling springs were invented in 14th century Europe.

PENDULUM

Pendulums consist of a suspended weight which swings back and forth on the end of a wire or rod. Italian scientist Galileo Galilei found that a pendulum always takes the same amount of time to complete its swing. The pendulum's regular movement was used by Dutch astronomer Christiaan Huygens in 1656 to build more accurate clocks. At the time, mechanical clocks could run 15–30 minutes out of time each day. Huygens' pendulum clock reduced the error to mere seconds. Further improvements made pendulum clocks the world's most accurate timepieces until the invention of quartz and electric clocks in the 1930s.

MOUSE

During the 1960s, American computing visionary Douglas Engelbart was testing out user-friendly ways of controlling cursors on computer screens. He developed a small box, called a mouse for its long tail-like cable, with metal wheels at right angles to each other. As the box moved around a desk, the wheels turned and sent signals to move the screen cursor the desired distance and direction. Engelbart's colleague William English built a prototype with a wooden case and single button in 1963. Later versions were molded from plastic with wheels replaced by a rolling ball. Eventually, millions of mice would be sold.

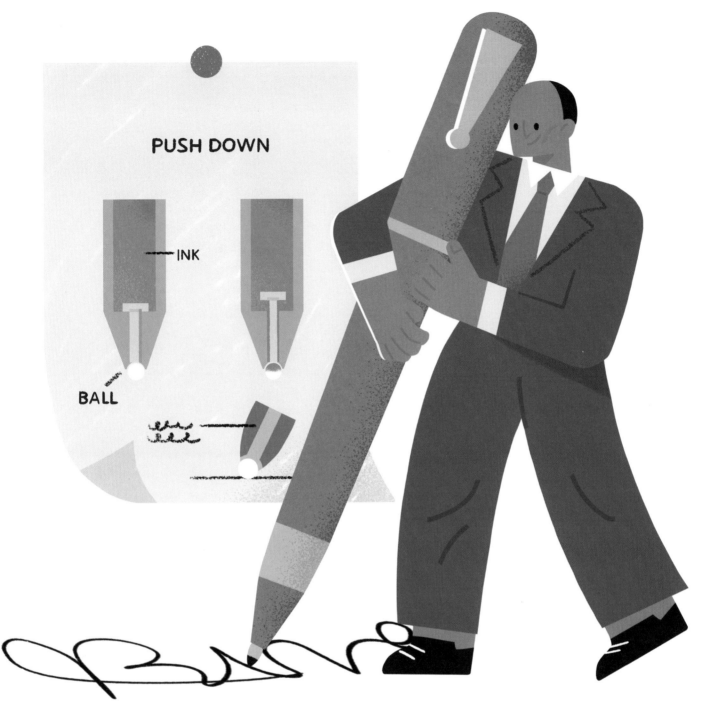

BALLPOINT

American John J. Loud patented a ballpoint pen design in 1888 but never capitalized on his invention. It would be 50 years before Hungarian journalist László Bíró developed his own pen, with a tiny metal ball at its tip. As the pen moved across the paper, the ball turned, picking up thick, quick-drying ink from the cartridge inside. On its launch, people marveled at the pen's long life and the lack of leaks or ink smudges. Bíró licensed his design to other pen makers, one of whom, Frenchman Marcel Bich, sold over 100 billion of his disposable BIC Cristal pens.

SATELLITE

Launched into space on the top of a converted missile, the Soviet Union's *Sputnik 1* caused a sensation in 1957. The beachball-sized device orbited Earth more than 1,400 times—becoming the world's first artificial satellite. Inside the metal sphere, three large batteries powered a radio transmitter which sent constant signals back to Earth. Amateur radio enthusiasts were able to track *Sputnik's* progress across the sky. Thousands of satellites have since followed *Sputnik*, performing a range of valuable jobs. These include taking images of Earth, mapping weather systems, and relaying TV and other communication signals between different points on the planet.

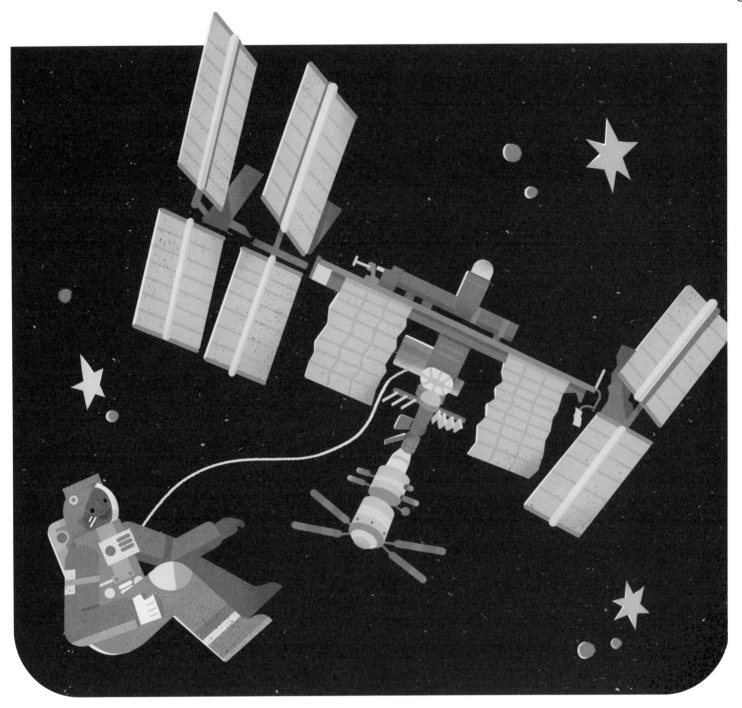

SPACE STATION

Until the invention of space stations, astronauts could only spend days in space.
Space stations orbit Earth for months or years at a time, providing a long-term
home. The Soviet Union launched the first of six Salyut space stations in 1971. Early
craft were launched as a whole, but from 1998 the International Space Station (ISS) was
put together in space, module-by-module. As long as a football field, the ISS has
as much living space as a five bedroom house. It contains gym equipment, two toilets
but no shower, and has been home to over 240 astronauts from 19 countries.

CINEMA

In 1895, the world's first cinema audience assembled at the Grand Café in Paris. There, they were amazed by ten black and white films, each under a minute long. These moving pictures or movies were the work of French brothers Auguste and Louis Lumière, using their Cinématographe machine. It recorded 16 photographs a second, onto long spools of celluloid film. The device ingeniously doubled as a projector, using a lantern to project the images onto a wall or screen so many could watch at once. When displayed quickly one after the other, the images gave the illusion of realistic movement.

SMELL-O-VISION

Some inventions seem like a good idea at the time! In the 1950s, TV was booming and cinemas were seeking exciting ways to attract back large audiences. Hans E. Laube created a system of electric fans and hundreds of yards of tubing, which wafted different smells to each cinema-goer's seat. Some 30 smells, including baked bread, sea air, oranges, and roses were each released to coincide with a particular moment in a film. A big budget movie, *Scent of Mystery*, was produced in 1960 to showcase Smell-O-Vision alongside plans for 100 smelly cinemas, but the pricey invention didn't catch on!

TESLA

EDISON

AC

· ·

Electricity can either flow as direct current (DC) or alternating current (AC). In 1882, Thomas Edison built pioneering DC power stations in London and New York, but the electricity supplied could only travel short distances. Serbian engineer Nikola Tesla developed the technology to generate and distribute AC electricity. This could travel farther, meaning that fewer power stations had to be built to supply a city. Tesla was backed by businessman George Westinghouse and fought a "War of the Currents" with Edison during the 1880s. AC power won out and is still how mains electricity is supplied around the modern world.

TURBINE

· ·

Wind has been used for centuries to power windmills, to grind cereal crops or to pump water. In the 1880s, two men invented wind-driven turbines, which powered generators to produce clean, green electricity without any pollution. Scotsman James Blyth built a 33-foot-tall turbine that helped light his holiday home. American engineer Charles Brush's 144-blade turbine was then built the following year. In Denmark, Paul LaCour developed four-bladed turbines to supply electricity to small villages in the 1890s. Hundreds were built. Today, multiple turbines are often grouped together in wind farms with wind power producing nearly 5% of the world's electricity.

VELCRO®

Once when out walking, Swiss electrical engineer George de Mestral was puzzled by why so many sticky burrs from plants stuck to clothing and his dog's fur. Viewing a burr under a microscope, he discovered its surface was a mass of tiny hooks, which caught in the loops of fabric and fur. After experimenting with various materials, de Mestral perfected pairs of fastening strips. One contained thousands of tiny hooks, and the other microscopic loops. Velcro® was launched in 1955 and used as handy fastenings on clothing, bags, and footwear—by 1960, over 50 million yards was produced a year.

TRAMPOLINE

A circus visit in 1930 inspired 16-year-old gymnast George Nissen to mimic the safety net used beneath trapeze artists. He invented his own "bouncing rig" in his parents' garage, using a canvas sheet attached to an iron frame with tire inner tubes. While at university, Nissen worked with his gym coach to refine the design, using springs instead of tubes. Trampolines went on sale in 1942, creating a new sport and a popular hobby. Nissen isn't the only notable young inventor. Britain's Peter Chilvers was 12 when he invented the windsurfer, and ice pop inventor Frank Epperson was just 11!

TELEPHONE

In 1861, Germany's Johann Philipp Reis turned sounds into electrical signals that could be sent along wires, and then converted to sound at the other end. He tested his telephone with a nonsense sentence, "The horse does not eat cucumber salad!" However, he didn't develop this device further. A decade later, Elisha Gray, Antonio Meucci, and Alexander Graham Bell all raced to build and patent a practical telephone. Bell got there first in 1876, sparking a 20 year-long legal battle. During that time, hundreds of thousands of telephones were installed allowing people to speak instantly to others over long distances.

HEADPHONES

Headphones contain small loudspeakers. These take electrical signals from a sound source and vibrate the speaker's diaphragm to create sound waves. A single, heavy speaker worn on one ear was first used by telephonists in the 1880s. In 1910, American Nathaniel Baldwin developed comfortable twin-speaker headphones. On receiving a US Navy order for 100 pairs, Baldwin built them on his kitchen table! Advances saw the first stereo headphones in 1958 and the first truly wireless in-ear headphones, the Onkyo W800BT, in 2015. In between, Dr. Amar Bose invented noise-canceling headphones that remove background sounds to create an immersive listening environment.

DISHWASHER

Annoyed at how her fine china plates were sometimes chipped when washed up by hand, Josephine Cochran set out to solve the problem. The American housewife developed a machine fitted with wire baskets to hold her prized crockery. The baskets were placed inside a copper boiler on a wheel, turned by hand or motor. As the wheel rotated the crockery, it was cleaned by jets of hot water from the boiler. Gaining a patent in 1886, Cochran formed a company and sold her invention to local restaurants and hotels. One of her larger models washed 240 dishes in two minutes!

SLICED BREAD

··

US jewelery shop owner Otto Rohwedder was serious about sliced bread! He placed newspaper ads asking people to tell him their ideal thickness of a slice of bread. He received over 30,000 replies. By 1912 he had built a prototype of his loaf-slicing machine, but a factory fire in 1917 destroyed his plans. By the time he built a new and improved version in 1927, electric toasters were gaining popularity, making his invention even more popular. Rohwedder's automatic bread slicer used steel blades to cut loaves into even slices. By the mid-1930s, two-thirds of all American bread sold was pre-sliced.

PHONOGRAPH

With the words "Mary had a little lamb," Thomas Edison demonstrated the world's first sound recording and playback machine—the phonograph. Edison's 1877 invention gathered in sound waves, which travel as vibrations through the air. These moved a metal stylus which etched indentations into foil wrapped around a cylinder (later versions replaced the foil with wax). When replayed, the indentations caused a different stylus to vibrate and recreate the sound waves. In 1887, Emile Berliner's gramophone system recorded sounds onto flat discs instead of cylinders. These discs, later known as records, could be copied more easily and held longer recordings.

STREAMING

Streaming means receiving music or video in real time, as a constant flow of data over
a computer network. Before streaming, there were devices like the Telharmonium,
which played tunes down telephone lines to subscribers in New York, in the 1890s.
It wasn't until the 1990s that media was streamed widely over the Internet. In 1995,
a sports channel offered the first live streaming event—a radio commentary of a baseball
game. Faster Internet led to video sharing and streaming sites like YouTube, which began
in 2005 and now sees one billion hours of videos streamed and watched every day.

PLASTIC

Plastics are polymers—materials made from long chains of molecules. The first synthetic plastic was Bakelite, invented by Belgian chemist Leo Baekeland in 1907. Made cheaply from coal tar, Bakelite was easy to shape and was used widely in the electrical industry because it resisted both electricity and heat. Further research created new plastics, including polystyrene in 1929, polythene in 1933, and nylon in 1935. Plastics proved popular, versatile, cheap to produce, and durable. Most, however, take 450 years or more to biodegrade (break down in nature), which has proved to be a problem as levels of plastic waste rise.

BARBIE®

Many children in the 1950s played with baby dolls or with dolls made of paper. Instead, Ruth Handler created a 11.5-inch-tall, plastic model of a glamorous young woman, which could be dressed in many different themed outfits. Naming the figure after her daughter, Barbara, Handler launched Barbie® at the 1959 New York Toy Fair—351,000 dolls sold in the first year. Barbie's® boyfriend Ken was introduced in 1961, a talking Barbie® in 1968, and Hispanic and African-American Barbies® in 1980. Hundreds of outfits and accessories were produced. Today, around 100 iconic Barbies® are sold every minute in over 150 countries.

X-RAY

German scientist Wilhelm Conrad Röntgen was experimenting with light tubes in 1895, when he discovered mysterious waves of energy he called X-rays. These high-energy waves passed through skin, flesh, and soft parts of the body, but not through bone or metal. Röntgen placed his wife's hand between the X-rays and a photographic plate, to produce the first X-ray image (radiogram) of the inside of the human body. Radiography departments sprang up in the world's hospitals using X-rays to detect broken bones, lung infections, and other medical issues, saving many lives. X-rays are also used to investigate the structure of materials.

PHOTOVOLTAIC

· ·

In 1839, a 19-year-old Frenchman, Edmond Becquerel, discovered the photovoltaic effect—where sunlight striking certain materials generates an electric current. The first scientist to build a working photovoltaic cell was Charles Fritts in 1883. It was only 1% efficient, meaning that 99% of the energy available was lost. Ever since, many scientists and engineers have strived to create more productive photovoltaic cells. The first practical solar panels, filled with photovoltaic cells, powered space satellites from the late 1950s onward. Today, photovoltaic cells boast 20% or more efficiency. They generate around 3% of all the world's electricity, without polluting the environment.

WIPER

The inventor of the first windshield wiper had never driven a car! Mary Anderson was inspired by watching New York City drivers having to leave their vehicle to remove rain, dirt, and snow from their windshield. Anderson sketched a solution involving a single rubber wiper blade on a steel arm. It traveled across the windshield when a lever was moved by hand inside the car. She received a US patent in 1903 but it was not a commercial success. Fourteen years later, another American woman, Charlotte Bridgwood, invented the first electric automatic wipers, which used cleaning rollers instead of blades.

CAT'S EYE

In 1934, Englishman Percy Shaw invented an ingeniously simple solution to a serious road safety problem. On dark or foggy twisting roads without street lighting, it could be difficult for motorists to stay safely in their lane. To reduce crashes and accidents, Shaw encased four glass beads inside a flexible rubber dome with a steel base. These reflecting road studs, nicknamed cat's eyes, were fitted every few paces along the middle of a road. The glass beads reflected vehicle headlights and marked out the two sides of the road, without needing a power source. Millions have been manufactured ever since.

BARCODE

Barcodes are a series of parallel thick and thin lines, which can be scanned and read by a machine, like a checkout scanner. The lines represent a unique code number, which identifies the product and allows computers to track sales, stock, and delivery. The idea for barcodes came to young engineer Joe Woodland on Miami Beach in 1949, while he was tracing lines in the sand with his fingers. It took advances in computing and lasers before a practical system was created by George Laurer in 1974. The system's first scan, a pack of chewing gum, began the barcode era!

LASER

Lasers are narrow, concentrated beams of light, which can travel long distances without spreading out. In 1960, American engineer Theodore H. Maiman used the burst of light from a photography flash lamp to excite the atoms in a rod of ruby crystal. The atoms produced a stream of energy, which escaped the rod as the very first laserlight. Different lasers have since been produced to perform hundreds of tasks. Some safely scan barcodes and DVDs or produce light shows. Other powerful lasers cut materials accurately. Medical lasers are used in eye operations and to seal blood vessels during surgery.

AUTHOR'S NOTE

Phew! That was quite some journey, from the first plows, to the latest computers and 3D printers. I hope you enjoyed learning about all the amazing inventions and their equally astonishing inventors.

Picking just 100 inventions was really hard as there are hundreds more with equally incredible stories to tell. Of those you read about, what were your favorites and which surprised you the most? Which invention do you feel has made the most impact? Was there one invention you wish *you* had invented or one inventor you would most like to meet?

As a bit of a tinkerer myself, I love the fact that you're never too young or too old to invent. In fact, you can start right now! What problem would you seek to solve with your invention? How would you design and build it?

Get thinking and sketching ... and good luck!

Clive Gifford

YOUNG INVENTORS

Alexander Graham Bell didn't just invent telephones. His other innovations include hydrofoils for fast boats and some of the first ever metal detectors. His first invention at the age of 12 was a rotating set of brushes which removed the husks from wheat and was used in a neighbor's flour mill. Many inventors start young. Here are four notable examples.

BLAISE PASCAL

This French child prodigy was brilliant at math and was correcting his father's accounts before he was a teenager. To help his father with his work as a tax collector, Pascal invented one of the first practical mechanical calculators in 1642 at the age of 18.

CHESTER GREENWOOD

After finding scarves wrapped around his ears failed to keep him warm in winter, 15-year-old Chester Greenwood tried something different. In 1873, he built a wire frame and attached pads made of warm beaver skin to invent the first ever earmuffs. Greenwood went on to sell hundreds of thousands and also invented new types of rakes, spark plugs, and fold-up beds!

JOSEPH-ARMAND BOMBARDIER

In 1922, this 15 year old who loved to experiment, mounted a Model T Ford car engine onto four wooden runners as skis. The engine turned a propeller to send Bombardier's newly invented snowmobile whizzing forward on snow.

DEEPIKA KURUP

On a trip to India, Kurup was shocked to see children drinking dirty water and vowed to do something about it. A keen child chemist, she invented a purifying material which removed bacteria from water when it was activated by sunlight. At the age of 14, she won the America's Top Young Scientist 2012 prize.

RUMAAN MALIK

In 2018, this 11-year-old English schoolgirl invented the Alarm Cup. This ingenious fruit bowl is designed to cut down food waste. It has a small touchscreen which can remind people when time is running out to eat the fruit before it starts to rot.

TIMELINE

Around 5500 BCE
The first plows are invented to dig up hard soil and make planting crops easier.

Around 3500 BCE
The date given for the first ancient Greek Olympic Games.

2000–1500 BCE
The ancient Egyptians invent a number of useful tools, including scissors, saws, and the lock and key.

around 1200 BCE
The Iron Age begins with people using this versatile metal to fashion strong tools and objects.

Around 750 BCE
The Assyrians invent the pulley—a device that makes lifting and pulling easier and is later found on cranes and other machines.

Around 260 BCE
Greek thinker Archimedes describes how levers work. Levers are found in hundreds of different devices.

104 CE
First documented details of paper's invention in ancient China.

231 CE
The wheelbarrow is invented in China.

1450s
Movable type printing press appears in Europe, helping spread news and printed information more widely than before.

1609
The first telescopes are invented by Dutch lens makers and quickly improved by European scientists, including Galileo Galilei.

1656
Dutch scientist Christiaan Huygens invents the pendulum clock—more accurate than earlier timepieces.

1765
James Watt's improvements to the steam engine help spark their widespread use in industry and, later, as locomotives on train lines.

1783
The Montgolfier brothers invent the first hot-air balloon capable of carrying human passengers.

1804
Richard Trevithick demonstrates the first steam locomotive able to pull wagons along railway tracks.

1830s
The first telegraph systems are invented. For the first time, messages can be sent long distances, along wires, reaching their destination in seconds.

1847
Thomas Edison is born. This American became one of the world's most prolific inventors with major contributions in lighting, electricity generation, sound, and vision.

1856
English engineer Henry Bessemer invents a process for making good quality steel cheaply. Steel becomes one of the most important materials.

1859
French scientist Gaston Planté invents the first rechargeable electric battery.

1876
Nikolaus Otto perfects a practical internal combustion engine—a type of engine that would later power cars, motorbikes, boats, and planes.

1876
Alexander Graham Bell is the first to patent a successful, working telephone system.

1885
Carl Benz invents the first practical motor car powered by an internal combustion engine.

1890
The first automatic telephone exchange is invented by Almon Strowger and speeded up phone call connections.

1903
The Wright brothers fly the first heavier-than-air craft, ushering in the era of aviation.

1930s
Many new and useful plastics are developed during this decade, including Neoprene and Nylon.

1937
The first jet engines are invented in Germany by Hans von Ohain and in Britain by Frank Whittle.

1940s
The first electronic digital computers are built during World War II. These machines filled entire rooms and performed complex math calculations.

1947
Three US engineers—John Bardeen, Walter Brattain, and William Shockley—demonstrate the first transistor. This small electrical component led to a boom in inventions in electronics.

1957
The Soviet Union kicks off the race into space by launching the world's first successful artificial satellite, Sputnik.

1960
US scientist Theodore H. Maiman invents the first working laser.

1961
The first robot to work for a living enters a US car factory, invented by George Devol and Joseph Engelberger.

1970
The first electronic pocket calculators are invented in Japan.

1975
The first working digital camera is invented by US engineer Steve Sasson.

1981
The first commercially available mountain bike, the Specialized Stumpjumper, goes on sale.

1991
Tim Berners-Lee gets the World Wide Web up and running, sparking a revolution in websites and online information.

1998
The first module of the International Space Station is launched into space.

2002
The first Roomba robot vacuum cleaner is invented by the iRobot company.

2010s
3D printing becomes affordable and popular for many, including budding inventors.

GLOSSARY

artificial made or produced by people and not found in nature.

automated when a task or process is carried out by machines without humans being heavily involved.

BCE short for Before Common Era, it follows a year date and refers to any point in history before the birth of Jesus Christ. So 100 BCE is three hundred years before 200 CE.

hydrogen the lightest chemical element—a substance made of just one type of atom.

internet a global network of computer networks through which computers communicate by sending information.

molecule made of atoms, this is the smallest unit of a substance that can be identified.

orbiting when one object travels in a circular or elliptical path around another body in space such as the Moon or a satellite orbiting Earth or Earth orbiting the Sun.

patent a right granted to an inventor by a government which stops others copying the invention for a set period of time.

programmed to provide a computer or another device with a series of coded instructions.

prototype an experimental design of part or all of an invention built for testing.

Soviet Union short for the Union of Soviet Socialist Republics (USSR), this large nation existed from 1922 until 1991 when it split up into Russia and 14 other countries.

INDEX

FIND OUT MORE

Books

The Story of Inventions, Catherine Barr (Frances Lincoln Children's Books, 2020)
Invented by Animals, Christiane Dorion (Wide-Eyed Editions, 2021)
Girls Think of Everything: Stories of Ingenious Inventions by Women, Catherine Thimmesh (Houghton Mifflin, 2018)
This Book Thinks You're an Inventor, Jon Milton (Thames and Hudson, 2020)
Science Museum: The Book of Inventions: Discover Brilliant Ideas from Fascinating People, Tim Cooke (Welbeck Children's, 2020)

Websites

https://inventivekids.com/
This website has lots of fun profiles of inventors and inventions, and tips on inventing your own creations.

https://www.history.com/topics/inventions
Lots of articles and videos on famous inventors and inventions from history.

https://www.timeforkids.com/g56/topics/inventions/
The kids' pages of *Time* magazine contain lots of fascinating news stories and collections of the best inventions of each year.

https://lemelson.mit.edu/resources/inventor-archive
A large archive of profiles of mostly US inventors, searchable alphabetically.